It's all about Faith
Daniel chapter 1
Good morning from ,

I am having computer trouble so this lesson may be a bit late. This old PC is wearing out and refuses to do the simple task required. Like all of us old things it is just so far behind the times it can no longer keep up. Nevertheless we will do as best we can.
So, we are now in study in the book of Daniel and like other books we have studied together I find myself excited about the coming events we will be reading about
Believe it or not there is a great deal of controversy about this book of Daniel. It is believed this book was written in the Babylonian and Persian period in or near the city of Babylon. However some noted scholars believe the book was not written in Babylon, but in Palestine. Some believe it was written after the fact and is history instead of Prophecy. However scrolls found and printed in 1956 show Nebuchadnezzar to have been in Judah and taking prisoners into exile as in the

time period written by Daniel.
Also it is interesting to note that the prophet Jeremiah, Ezekiel and Daniel were all actively working for the Lord in about the same time period while in captivity in Babylon. A fact that I was not aware of until recently, (If we are to learn, we must study.)
This shows us that as determined, as the Israel people were to destroy themselves God was even more determined to save them. This brings the reader to wonder "just why bother", but we are speaking about God here and the only reason I can think of is because these were HIS people and HE loved them and was simply not going to let Satan (which is who the real culprit is here) destroy His work and people.
This brings me to this wondering thought. Will we find others who though not written about and made famous working just as hard for God? Perhaps not, but I believe they were there nonetheless.

OK, that was rather lengthy and quite honestly I have much more to say, but we must move on. In this first chapter of Daniel we find the story many of us remember even from our childhood. I recall the Baptist preacher standing in the pulpit holding the bible up and walking back and forth speaking of Daniel as a young boy in captivity there in Babylon with his friends and of the king asking for several of those children who had learned their lessons well in Israel to be taken by his chief eunuch Melzar and trained in the ways of the king for three years and then to stand in audience before him.

Now Daniel and his three friends ,Hananiah, and Mishael, and Azariah, who we know as Shadrach, Meshach, and Abednego were chosen and taken along with several others to be given training and in doing so would receive the very best food and wine as was possible. They were in essence to eat the same food that was prepared for the king himself.

Daniel and I suppose the other boys decided not to defile themselves with this food from the kings table and Daniel ask Melzar to allow them to eat other things. I believe we find this to be mainly vegetables and such.

I will stop here because this chapter is self-explaining and you need to learn for

yourselves by reading the words written so long ago. It will give you the bigger picture and allow you to know God.
I will see you tomorrow if this PC will allow it.
It just takes a tiny spark to lite a candle and if everyone were to lite but one little what a bright world this would be.
Peace.

Chapter 1
Daniel and his friends obey God

1 In the third year of the reign of Jehoiakim king of Judah came Nebuchadnezzar king of Babylon unto Jerusalem, and besieged it.
2 And the Lord gave Jehoiakim king of Judah into his hand, with part of the vessels of the house of God: which he carried into the land of Shinar to the house of his god; and he brought the vessels into the treasure house of his god.
3 And the king spake unto Ashpenaz the master of his eunuchs, that he should bring certain of the children of Israel, and of the king's seed, and of the princes;

4 Children in whom was no blemish, but well favoured, and skilful in all wisdom, and cunning in knowledge, and understanding science, and such as had ability in them to stand in the king's palace, and whom they might teach the learning and the tongue of the Chaldeans.

5 And the king appointed them a daily provision of the king's meat, and of the wine which he drank: so nourishing them three years, that at the end thereof they might stand before the king.

6 Now among these were of the children of Judah, Daniel, Hananiah, Mishael, and Azariah:

7 Unto whom the prince of the eunuchs gave names: for he gave unto Daniel the name of Belteshazzar; and to Hananiah, of Shadrach; and to Mishael, of Meshach; and to Azariah, of Abednego.

8 But Daniel purposed in his heart that he would not defile himself with the portion of the king's meat, nor with the wine which he drank: therefore he requested of the prince of the eunuchs that he might not defile himself.

9 Now God had brought Daniel into favour and tender love with the prince of the eunuchs.
10 And the prince of the eunuchs said unto Daniel, I fear my lord the king, who hath appointed your meat and your drink: for why should he see your faces worse liking than the children which are of your sort? Then shall ye make me endanger my head to the king.
11 Then said Daniel to Melzar, whom the prince of the eunuchs had set over Daniel, Hananiah, Mishael, and Azariah,
12 Prove thy servants, I beseech thee, ten days; and let them give us pulse to eat, and water to drink.
13 Then let our countenances be looked upon before thee, and the countenance of the children that eat of the portion of the king's meat: and as thou seest, deal with thy servants.
14 So he consented to them in this matter, and proved them ten days.
15 And at the end of ten days their countenances appeared fairer and fatter in flesh than all the children which did eat the portion of the king's meat.

16 Thus Melzar took away the portion of their meat, and the wine that they should drink; and gave them pulse.

17 As for these four children, God gave them knowledge and skill in all learning and wisdom: and Daniel had understanding in all visions and dreams.

18 Now at the end of the days that the king had said he should bring them in, then the prince of the eunuchs brought them in before Nebuchadnezzar.

19 And the king communed with them; and among them all was found none like Daniel, Hananiah, Mishael, and Azariah: therefore stood they before the king.

20 And in all matters of wisdom and understanding, that the king enquired of them, he found them ten times better than all the magicians and astrologers that were in all his realm.

21 And Daniel continued even unto the first year of king Cyrus.

It's all about Faith
Daniel chapter 2
Good morning from Arizona

Wednesday morning and I am reminded of a very funny commercial I saw on TV recently where a camel comes into an office setting and demands to know what day it is. Of course referring to "Hump" day or the middle of the week day. Very funny.

OK, that is enough of me for now. We study this morning in the 2nd chapter of the book of Daniel and it is really quite involved at first glance. However we will make the events unfold in a manner that hopefully makes it a bit easier to understand.
this is about the dream Nebuchadnezzar had and needs an explanation for. The dream frightened him and he called all of his wise men together and demanded to know what the dream meant promising them two things. If they could tell him of the dream they would receive wealth and gifts, but if they could not they would be put to death. Notice this is complete power of the king. When he spoke that was it. No question; a very scary situation. These people he called together were Sorcerers (people that cast spells and such) Chaldeans, classes of wise men (people who were there to support the king and it is interesting to note that

these people were descendants from Abraham's nephew) it is inferred that Nebuchadnezzar was from these people as well

The king said to these men that he had forgotten the dream because I believe he wanted to see if they really could tell him what it was about. I will pause here and share with you that this chapter is very clear in its writing and reads like a story or fairy tale, but we must realize it is real and is history we need to know

Excuses were made by these wise man and the king became angry telling his chief guard to take them all (including Daniel and his friends) and kill them.

The chief guard came to Daniel and explained his situation and Daniel told the man to take him to the king.

Once in front of the king Daniel began telling him of the dream of this figure he saw in a dream and that it explained the future kings and kingdoms to follow.

I will skip forward here and share the legs of iron and feet of iron and clay. The iron represents the Roman Empire and the feet mixed with iron and clay represents the weakness of that empire in its final days. A remnant of which we still have today, referring to the Catholic Church. Daniel explains to the king (again) so the king can understand, and this is Gods doing because unless he did understand this difficult dream Daniel and the rest of them would have been killed.

The king was so overcome that he fell on his face and then gave Daniel complete control of his kingdom. Daniel secured positions for his three friends then begins his new position complete with power and all that goes with it.

As you see there is much more to say about this chapter and in doing research I must tell you it could have gone on for days. I will tell you there is much controversy about the authenticity of this book by some historians.

Sadly, I must close for now.

It takes but a small spark to lite a candle, but if everyone would lite but one small candle what a bright world this would be. Until tomorrow then..

Chapter 2
Nebuchadnezzar's Dream

1 In the second year of his reign, Nebuchadnezzar had dreams; his mind

was troubled and he could not sleep.
2 So the king summoned the magicians, enchanters, sorcerers and astrologers to tell him what he had dreamed. When they came in and stood before the king,
3 he said to them, "I have had a dream that troubles me and I want to know what it means."
4 Then the astrologers answered the king in Aramaic, "O king, live forever! Tell your servants the dream, and we will interpret it."
5 The king replied to the astrologers, "This is what I have firmly decided: If you do not tell me what my dream was and interpret it, I will have you cut into pieces and your houses turned into piles of rubble.
6 But if you tell me the dream and explain it, you will receive from me gifts and rewards and great honor. So tell me the dream and interpret it for me."
7 Once more they replied, "Let the king tell his servants the dream, and we will interpret it."
8 Then the king answered, "I am certain that you are trying to gain time, because you realize that this is what I have firmly decided:

9 If you do not tell me the dream, there is just one penalty for you. You have conspired to tell me misleading and wicked things, hoping the situation will change. So then, tell me the dream, and I will know that you can interpret it for me."
10 The astrologers answered the king, "There is not a man on earth who can do what the king asks! No king, however great and mighty, has ever asked such a thing of any magician or enchanter or astrologer.
11 What the king asks is too difficult. No one can reveal it to the king except the gods, and they do not live among men."
12 This made the king so angry and furious that he ordered the execution of all the wise men of Babylon.
13 So the decree was issued to put the wise men to death, and men were sent to look for Daniel and his friends to put them to death.
14 When Arioch, the commander of the king's guard, had gone out to put to death the wise men of Babylon, Daniel spoke to him with wisdom and tact.
15 He asked the king's officer, "Why did the king issue such a harsh decree?" Arioch then explained the matter to

Daniel.

16 At this, Daniel went in to the king and asked for time, so that he might interpret the dream for him.

17 Then Daniel returned to his house and explained the matter to his friends Hananiah, Mishael and Azariah.

18 He urged them to plead for mercy from the God of heaven concerning this mystery, so that he and his friends might not be executed with the rest of the wise men of Babylon.

19 During the night the mystery was revealed to Daniel in a vision. Then Daniel praised the God of heaven

20 and said: "Praise be to the name of God for ever and ever; wisdom and power are his.

21 He changes times and seasons; he sets up kings and deposes them. He gives wisdom to the wise and knowledge to the discerning.

22 He reveals deep and hidden things; he knows what lies in darkness, and light dwells with him.

23 I thank and praise you, O God of my fathers: You have given me wisdom and power, you have made known to me what we asked of you, you have made known

to us the dream of the king."

Daniel Explains the Dream

24 Then Daniel went to Arioch, whom the king had appointed to execute the wise men of Babylon, and said to him, "Do not execute the wise men of Babylon. Take me to the king, and I will interpret his dream for him."
25 Arioch took Daniel to the king at once and said, "I have found a man among the exiles from Judah who can tell the king what his dream means."
26 The king asked Daniel (also called Belteshazzar), "Are you able to tell me what I saw in my dream and interpret it?"
27 Daniel replied, "No wise man, enchanter, magician or diviner can explain to the king the mystery he has asked about,
28 but there is a God in heaven who reveals mysteries. He has shown King Nebuchadnezzar what will happen in days to come. Your dream and the visions that passed through your mind as you lay on your bed are these:
29 "As you were lying there, O king, your mind turned to things to come, and the

revealer of mysteries showed you what is going to happen.

30 As for me, this mystery has been revealed to me, not because I have greater wisdom than other living men, but so that you, O king, may know the interpretation and that you may understand what went through your mind.

31 "You looked, O king, and there before you stood a large statue--an enormous, dazzling statue, awesome in appearance.

32 The head of the statue was made of pure gold, its chest and arms of silver, its belly and thighs of bronze,

33 its legs of iron, its feet partly of iron and partly of baked clay.

34 While you were watching, a rock was cut out, but not by human hands. It struck the statue on its feet of iron and clay and smashed them.

35 Then the iron, the clay, the bronze, the silver and the gold were broken to pieces at the same time and became like chaff on a threshing floor in the summer. The wind swept them away without leaving a trace. But the rock that struck the statue became a huge mountain and filled the whole earth.

36 "This was the dream, and now we will

interpret it to the king.

37 You, O king, are the king of kings. The God of heaven has given you dominion and power and might and glory;

38 in your hands he has placed mankind and the beasts of the field and the birds of the air. Wherever they live, he has made you ruler over them all. You are that head of gold.

39 "After you, another kingdom will rise, inferior to yours. Next, a third kingdom, one of bronze, will rule over the whole earth.

40 Finally, there will be a fourth kingdom, strong as iron--for iron breaks and smashes everything--and as iron breaks things to pieces, so it will crush and break all the others.

41 Just as you saw that the feet and toes were partly of baked clay and partly of iron, so this will be a divided kingdom; yet it will have some of the strength of iron in it, even as you saw iron mixed with clay.

42 As the toes were partly iron and partly clay, so this kingdom will be partly strong and partly brittle.

43 And just as you saw the iron mixed with baked clay, so the people will be a mixture and will not remain united, any

more than iron mixes with clay.
44 "In the time of those kings, the God of heaven will set up a kingdom that will never be destroyed, nor will it be left to another people. It will crush all those kingdoms and bring them to an end, but it will itself endure forever.
45 This is the meaning of the vision of the rock cut out of a mountain, but not by human hands--a rock that broke the iron, the bronze, the clay, the silver and the gold to pieces. "The great God has shown the king what will take place in the future. The dream is true and the interpretation is trustworthy."
46 Then King Nebuchadnezzar fell prostrate before Daniel and paid him honor and ordered that an offering and incense be presented to him.
47 The king said to Daniel, "Surely your God is the God of gods and the Lord of kings and a revealer of mysteries, for you were able to reveal this mystery."
48 Then the king placed Daniel in a high position and lavished many gifts on him. He made him ruler over the entire province of Babylon and placed him in charge of all its wise men.
49 Moreover, at Daniel's request the king

appointed Shadrach, Meshach and Abednego administrators over the province of Babylon, while Daniel himself remained at the royal court.

It's all about Faith
Daniel chapter 3
Good morning from the land of cactus and sand

Saturday morning and I have had a couple of days of frustration over this computer as it went completely down. Had it not been for the fact that my son is a whiz with these things I would have been searching for a way to replace it. As I Have said in the past it is quite old and needs to be replaced, but we make do with what we have so here I sit once again doing my lesson for the day. God is indeed good.

OK, this morning we are reading in the book of Daniel chapter 3 and as I read this and did my research I was flooded with memories of my childhood. For as a youngster on Sunday morning my mother would put my sister and I on the old church bus and send us off to what she thought was church. However, our church was located in town and two blocks from a drug store that had a great soda fountain, so on occasion (at least until the druggist ran us out) we would slip away from the bus and head for the drug store. Once there we would sit on a counter stool and order what was then called a "Black Cow". This was a scoop or two of ice cream mixed with a layer of nuts, then a layer of chocolate, then more ice cream, nuts, and chocolate, and so on until the class was full. Paying for it with our church money(and this made it more delicious) we would slip back to church and just pass the collection plate to the next person when it came around. This confession just slipped in here. Back to work on this lesson.

Our church was Baptist and I do so remember the preacher flying back and forth on the platform with his long coat tails flying waving the bible in the air and preaching this chapter of Daniel. What a site he was with his gray striped trousers and that long coat.

King Nebuchadnezzar had built a very large statue (it is believed of himself) and called all of the important people from around his kingdom to come to the dedication. This included Shadrach, Mesach, and Abednego. When all were gathered before the king his "herald" (announcer) stood and told all who were there that when they heard music from many instruments they were to bow down and worship this statue. The music then sounded and all the people then bowed down; except three, Shadrach, Mesach, and Abednego. As it happened some of those that Daniel had saved after interrupting the king's dream went to the king and accused the three of not worshiping the statue.

In a rage the king called them over and asked why they did not bow down. He was told and boldly so that they worshipped only the true God and would not bow down.

The king ordered the furnace to be fired to seven times normal temperature and to put the three youths in to be burned alive. They were tied in the very clothes they had on and delivered to the furnace. However it was so hot those who had brought them to the mouth of the furnace perished from the heat. The three then fell into the fiery furnace as the king

watched.
Suddenly the king jumped up and called for the three to come out of the furnace to him. For he saw them not burn but walking around inside the furnace as if they were on an afternoon walk. Furthermore he witnessed a fourth person in the furnace.
Now, there has over the years been much to do about just who this was and it does make good material for preachers to speak on, but the truth is it doesn't matter who it was. Heavenly being is who it was! The king was so impressed with what he had seen that he admitted to the three their God was indeed the God of the earth and he promoted them to important positions in the province of Babylon.
Have a great weekend and I will see you on Monday.
If everyone would lite but one little candle what a bright world this would be.
Peace.

Daniel chapter 3
Shadrach, Meshach, and Abed'nego are cast into fiery furnace.

1 King Nebuchadnezzar made an image

of gold, whose height was sixty cubits and its breadth six cubits. He set it up on the plain of Dura, in the province of Babylon.

2 Then King Nebuchadnezzar sent to gather the satraps, the prefects, and the governors, the counselors, the treasurers, the justices, the magistrates, and all the officials of the provinces to come to the dedication of the image that King Nebuchadnezzar had set up.

3 Then the satraps, the prefects, and the governors, the counselors, the treasurers, the justices, the magistrates, and all the officials of the provinces gathered for the dedication of the image that King Nebuchadnezzar had set up. And they stood before the image that Nebuchadnezzar had set up.

4 And the herald proclaimed aloud, "You are commanded, O peoples, nations, and languages,

5 that when you hear the sound of the horn, pipe, lyre, trigon, harp, bagpipe, and every kind of music, you are to fall down and worship the golden image that King Nebuchadnezzar has set up.

6 And whoever does not fall down and worship shall immediately be cast into a

burning fiery furnace."

7 Therefore, as soon as all the peoples heard the sound of the horn, pipe, lyre, trigon, harp, bagpipe, and every kind of music, all the peoples, nations, and languages fell down and worshiped the golden image that King Nebuchadnezzar had set up.

8 Therefore at that time certain Chaldeans came forward and maliciously accused the Jews.

9 They declared to King Nebuchadnezzar, "O king, live forever!

10 You, O king, have made a decree, that every man who hears the sound of the horn, pipe, lyre, trigon, harp, bagpipe, and every kind of music, shall fall down and worship the golden image.

11 And whoever does not fall down and worship shall be cast into a burning fiery furnace. 12 There are certain Jews whom you have appointed over the affairs of the province of Babylon: Shadrach, Meshach, and Abednego. These men, O king, pay no attention to you; they do not serve your gods or worship the golden image that you have set up."

13 Then Nebuchadnezzar in furious rage commanded that Shadrach, Meshach,

and Abednego be brought. So they brought these men before the king.

14 Nebuchadnezzar answered and said to them, "Is it true, O Shadrach, Meshach, and Abednego, that you do not serve my gods or worship the golden image that I have set up? 15 Now if you are ready when you hear the sound of the horn, pipe, lyre, trigon, harp, bagpipe, and every kind of music, to fall down and worship the image that I have made, well and good. But if you do not worship, you shall immediately be cast into a burning fiery furnace. And who is the god who will deliver you out of my hands?"

16 Shadrach, Meshach, and Abednego answered and said to the king, "O Nebuchadnezzar, we have no need to answer you in this matter.

17 If this be so, our God whom we serve is able to deliver us from the burning fiery furnace, and he will deliver us out of your hand, O king.

18 But if not, be it known to you, O king, that we will not serve your gods or worship the golden image that you have set up."

19 Then Nebuchadnezzar was filled with fury, and the expression of his face was

changed against Shadrach, Meshach, and Abednego. He ordered the furnace heated seven times more than it was usually heated.

20 And he ordered some of the mighty men of his army to bind Shadrach, Meshach, and Abednego, and to cast them into the burning fiery furnace.

21 Then these men were bound in their cloaks, their tunics, their hats, and their other garments, and they were thrown into the burning fiery furnace.

22 Because the king's order was urgent and the furnace overheated, the flame of the fire killed those men who took up Shadrach, Meshach, and Abednego.

23 And these three men, Shadrach, Meshach, and Abednego, fell bound into the burning fiery furnace.

24 Then King Nebuchadnezzar was astonished and rose up in haste. He declared to his counselors, "Did we not cast three men bound into the fire?" They answered and said to the king, "True, O king."

25 He answered and said, "But I see four men unbound, walking in the midst of the fire, and they are not hurt; and the appearance of the fourth is like a son of

the gods."

26 Then Nebuchadnezzar came near to the door of the burning fiery furnace; he declared, "Shadrach, Meshach, and Abednego, servants of the Most High God, come out, and come here!" Then Shadrach, Meshach, and Abednego came out from the fire.

27 And the satraps, the prefects, the governors, and the king's counselors gathered together and saw that the fire had not had any power over the bodies of those men. The hair of their heads was not singed, their cloaks were not harmed, and no smell of fire had come upon them.

28 Nebuchadnezzar answered and said, "Blessed be the God of Shadrach, Meshach, and Abednego, who has sent his angel and delivered his servants, who trusted in him, and set aside the king's command, and yielded up their bodies rather than serve and worship any god except their own God.

29 Therefore I make a decree: Any people, nation, or language that speaks anything against the God of Shadrach, Meshach, and Abednego shall be torn limb from limb, and their houses laid in ruins, for there is no other god who is

able to rescue in this way."
30 Then the king promoted Shadrach, Meshach, and Abednego in the province of Babylon.

It's all about Faith
Daniel chapter 4
Good morning from our house

Well, here I sit with a brand new computer with all the bells and whistles. I remember when I bought my first computer and after turning it on I had to wait for five minutes for everything to load. The capacity was 1 gig and I kept wanting to kill it. Keep in mind that I drove a model "A" automobile and learned to read with "Dick & Jane". So be patient please.

OK, we are reading in the book of Daniel chapter 4. Nebuchadnezzar was resting in his house after all the successful wars fought and the massive building projects in Babylon and had a dream. He had apparently called all of his quack advisors together (who should have been dismissed long ago) and of course none of them could tell him what the dream

meant so he reluctantly called Daniel.
The king knew that Daniels god was all powerful, but the term "My God" could have meant any of the Gods he worshipped. He was after all a pagan and not Christian as was Daniel.

Coming before the king Daniel was told about the dream and instantly understood it, but was reluctant to tell its meaning to this man that had been so kind to him, and so he was troubled. The king seeing this encouraged him to speak and so Daniel told the king of his dream. "The tree...it is thou O king". And as we read Daniel went on to describe to the king the things that he would experience causing him to learn that God was indeed the only and all powerful God of all the Heaven and Earth.

The king was amazed and recognized the truth of Daniels words.

We will when necessary be chastised by the Lord but He will always love us and give us a chance to repent and return to him, even the evil man if he turns to God. Remember, it takes just a tiny spark to lite a candle and if everyone would lite but one little candle what a bright world this would be.

Until we meet again.

Daniel Chapter 4

Nebuchadnezzar acknowledges Gods eternal dominion he relates a dream, Daniel interprets it the dream fulfilled.

1King Nebuchadnezzar to all peoples, nations, and languages that dwell in all the earth: Peace be multiplied to you!
2 It has seemed good to me to show the signs and wonders that the Most High God has done for me.
3 How great are his signs, how mighty his wonders! His kingdom is an everlasting kingdom, and his dominion endures from generation to generation.
4 I, Nebuchadnezzar, was at ease in my house and prospering in my palace.
5 I saw a dream that made me afraid. As I lay in bed the fancies and the visions of my head alarmed me.
6 So I made a decree that all the wise men of Babylon should be brought before me, that they might make known to me the interpretation of the dream.
7 Then the magicians, the enchanters, the Chaldeans, and the astrologers came in, and I told them the dream, but they

could not make known to me its interpretation.

8 At last Daniel came in before me—he who was named Belteshazzar after the name of my god, and in whom is the spirit of the holy gods—and I told him the dream, saying,

9 "O Belteshazzar, chief of the magicians, because I know that the spirit of the holy gods is in you and that no mystery is too difficult for you, tell me the visions of my dream that I saw and their interpretation.

10 The visions of my head as I lay in bed were these: I saw, and behold, a tree in the midst of the earth, and its height was great.

11 The tree grew and became strong, and its top reached to heaven, and it was visible to the end of the whole earth.

12 Its leaves were beautiful and its fruit abundant, and in it was food for all. The beasts of the field found shade under it, and the birds of the heavens lived in its branches, and all flesh was fed from it.

13 "I saw in the visions of my head as I lay in bed, and behold, a watcher, a holy one, came down from heaven.

14 He proclaimed aloud and said thus: 'Chop down the tree and lop off its

branches, strip off its leaves and scatter its fruit. Let the beasts flee from under it and the birds from its branches.

15 But leave the stump of its roots in the earth, bound with a band of iron and bronze, amid the tender grass of the field. Let him be wet with the dew of heaven. Let his portion be with the beasts in the grass of the earth.

16 Let his mind be changed from a man's, and let a beast's mind be given to him; and let seven periods of time pass over him.

17 The sentence is by the decree of the watchers, the decision by the word of the holy ones, to the end that the living may know that the Most High rules the kingdom of men and gives it to whom he will and sets over it the lowliest of men.'

18 This dream I, King Nebuchadnezzar, saw. And you, O Belteshazzar, tell me the interpretation, because all the wise men of my kingdom are not able to make known to me the interpretation, but you are able, for the spirit of the holy gods is in you."

19 Then Daniel, whose name was Belteshazzar, was dismayed for a while, and his thoughts alarmed him. The king

answered and said, "Belteshazzar, let not the dream or the interpretation alarm you." Belteshazzar answered and said, "My lord, may the dream be for those who hate you and its interpretation for your enemies!

20 The tree you saw, which grew and became strong, so that its top reached to heaven, and it was visible to the end of the whole earth,

21 whose leaves were beautiful and its fruit abundant, and in which was food for all, under which beasts of the field found shade, and in whose branches the birds of the heavens lived—

22 it is you, O king, who have grown and become strong. Your greatness has grown and reaches to heaven, and your dominion to the ends of the earth.

23 And because the king saw a watcher, a holy one, coming down from heaven and saying, 'Chop down the tree and destroy it, but leave the stump of its roots in the earth, bound with a band of iron and bronze, in the tender grass of the field, and let him be wet with the dew of heaven, and let his portion be with the beasts of the field, till seven periods of time pass over him,'

24 this is the interpretation, O king: It is a decree of the Most High, which has come upon my lord the king,
25 that you shall be driven from among men, and your dwelling shall be with the beasts of the field. You shall be made to eat grass like an ox, and you shall be wet with the dew of heaven, and seven periods of time shall pass over you, till you know that the Most High rules the kingdom of men and gives it to whom he will.
26 And as it was commanded to leave the stump of the roots of the tree, your kingdom shall be confirmed for you from the time that you know that Heaven rules.
27 Therefore, O king, let my counsel be acceptable to you: break off your sins by practicing righteousness, and your iniquities by showing mercy to the oppressed, that there may perhaps be a lengthening of your prosperity."
28 All this came upon King Nebuchadnezzar.
29 At the end of twelve months he was walking on the roof of the royal palace of Babylon, 30 and the king answered and said, "Is not this great Babylon, which I have built by my mighty power as a royal

residence and for the glory of my majesty?"

31 While the words were still in the king's mouth, there fell a voice from heaven, "O King Nebuchadnezzar, to you it is spoken: The kingdom has departed from you,

32 and you shall be driven from among men, and your dwelling shall be with the beasts of the field. And you shall be made to eat grass like an ox, and seven periods of time shall pass over you, until you know that the Most High rules the kingdom of men and gives it to whom he will."

33 Immediately the word was fulfilled against Nebuchadnezzar. He was driven from among men and ate grass like an ox, and his body was wet with the dew of heaven till his hair grew as long as eagles' feathers, and his nails were like birds' claws.

34 At the end of the days I, Nebuchadnezzar, lifted my eyes to heaven, and my reason returned to me, and I blessed the Most High, and praised and honored him who lives forever, for his dominion is an everlasting dominion, and his kingdom endures from generation to

generation;
35 all the inhabitants of the earth are accounted as nothing, and he does according to his will among the host of heaven and among the inhabitants of the earth; and none can stay his hand or say to him, "What have you done?"
36 At the same time my reason returned to me, and for the glory of my kingdom, my majesty and splendor returned to me. My counselors and my lords sought me, and I was established in my kingdom, and still more greatness was added to me.
37 Now I, Nebuchadnezzar, praise and extol and honor the King of heaven, for all his works are right and his ways are just; and those who walk in pride he is able to humble.

It's all about Faith
Daniel chapter 5
Good morning from the desert of southwestern America

Tuesday morning and here I sit once again doing Gods work at 4 in the morning. A new computer sits before me and I must tell you using a lap top is quite different than my old standby. Just can't seem to get used to this keyboard being just a bit out of reach, but things evolve and I will get used to holding my elbows up in time.

OK, today as we read in chapter 5 we make a change in direction and though we are still in the study and reading of Daniel the characters in the plot have changed a bit. It seems that Nebuchadnezzar while still king had not fared well in his battle with Cyrus armies and just now was under siege some miles away from home. This prince (who is really a pipsqueak of a man) Belshazzar is said to be a son of the great king but it has been found there is some evidence to the contrary. His biological father might well have been another. Nevertheless the king was away and this Belshazzar had thrown a party in the palace at the very time when Gobryas (A general of the Cyrus army) was at the gate of the city Babylon. It seems he had diverted the river and was just now leading his army up the riverbed toward the city. The river gates had been left unguarded and this was to be the entrance by which the invading army would enter the city.

Now when Belshazzar had invited the thousand guests to the feast he had sat with them and drank with them (This practice was unusual because the custom was that royalty would be behind drapes in that time of history.) and after a while ordered those vessels of gold, silver, and iron, which Nebuchadnezzar had taken from the Temple of the Lord to be brought forth and used for their pleasure of drinking. After having done so, there came in Belshazzar's sight a hand that began writing on the wall of the banquet room. Belshazzar sent for the wise men and told them if they could tell him what the words meant that person would be the third ruler of the kingdom. (He had no authority for this, but the king was gone and so for a short while he was the cock of the walk.) None could tell him what the words meant so the queen came in (This was not his wife nor mother but most likely his grandmother and told him of Daniel and his wisdom.) The prince sent for Daniel and offered him the third ruler of the kingdom as well, but Daniel refused and told the prince what the words meant. MENE, MENE, TEKEL, UPHARSIN were the words and this was their meaning.

(There is however some difference of opinion here.) MENE means God has numbered thy kingdom and finished it. TEKEL thou art weighed in the balance and found wanting. PERES, thy kingdom is divided and given to the Medes and Persians. The king heard it and dressed Daniel in purple and gave him a third of the kingdom. In that very night the prince was slain and the kingdom fell.

We might note here that Babylon was a fortress of incredible strength and had at that time enough food storage to last for twenty years. Yet something as simple as an unguarded gate caused her downfall. If everyone would lite but one little candle what a bright world this would be.

Until tomorrow then.

Chapter 5
The Hand Writing on the Wall

1 Belshazzar the king made a great feast to a thousand of his lords, and drank wine before the thousand.

2 Belshazzar, whiles he tasted the wine, commanded to bring the golden and silver vessels which his father Nebuchadnezzar had taken out of the

temple which was in Jerusalem; that the king, and his princes, his wives, and his concubines, might drink therein.

3 Then they brought the golden vessels that were taken out of the temple of the house of God which was at Jerusalem; and the king, and his princes, his wives, and his concubines, drank in them.

4 They drank wine, and praised the gods of gold, and of silver, of brass, of iron, of wood, and of stone.

5 In the same hour came forth fingers of a man's hand, and wrote over against the candlestick upon the plaister of the wall of the king's palace: and the king saw the part of the hand that wrote.

6 Then the king's countenance was changed, and his thoughts troubled him, so that the joints of his loins were loosed, and his knees smote one against another.

7 The king cried aloud to bring in the astrologers, the Chaldeans, and the soothsayers. And the king spake, and said to the wise men of Babylon, Whosoever shall read this writing, and shew me the interpretation thereof, shall be clothed with scarlet, and have a chain of gold about his neck, and shall be the third ruler in the kingdom.

8 Then came in all the king's wise men: but they could not read the writing, nor make known to the king the interpretation thereof.

9 Then was king Belshazzar greatly troubled, and his countenance was changed in him, and his lords were astonied.

10 Now the queen by reason of the words of the king and his lords came into the banquet house: and the queen spake and said, O king, live for ever: let not thy thoughts trouble thee, nor let thy countenance be changed:

11 There is a man in thy kingdom, in whom is the spirit of the holy gods; and in the days of thy father light and understanding and wisdom, like the wisdom of the gods, was found in him; whom the king Nebuchadnezzar thy father, the king, I say, thy father, made master of the magicians, astrologers, Chaldeans, and soothsayers;

12 Forasmuch as an excellent spirit, and knowledge, and understanding, interpreting of dreams, and shewing of hard sentences, and dissolving of doubts, were found in the same Daniel, whom the king named Belteshazzar: now let Daniel

be called, and he will shew the interpretation.

13 Then was Daniel brought in before the king. And the king spake and said unto Daniel, Art thou that Daniel, which art of the children of the captivity of Judah, whom the king my father brought out of Jewry?

14 I have even heard of thee, that the spirit of the gods is in thee, and that light and understanding and excellent wisdom is found in thee.

15 And now the wise men, the astrologers, have been brought in before me, that they should read this writing, and make known unto me the interpretation thereof: but they could not shew the interpretation of the thing:

16 And I have heard of thee, that thou canst make interpretations, and dissolve doubts: now if thou canst read the writing, and make known to me the interpretation thereof, thou shalt be clothed with scarlet, and have a chain of gold about thy neck, and shalt be the third ruler in the kingdom.

17 Then Daniel answered and said before the king, Let thy gifts be to thyself, and give thy rewards to another; yet I will read

the writing unto the king, and make known to him the interpretation.

18 O thou king, the most high God gave Nebuchadnezzar thy father a kingdom, and majesty, and glory, and honour:

19 And for the majesty that he gave him, all people, nations, and languages, trembled and feared before him: whom he would he slew; and whom he would he kept alive; and whom he would he set up; and whom he would he put down.

20 But when his heart was lifted up, and his mind hardened in pride, he was deposed from his kingly throne, and they took his glory from him:

21 And he was driven from the sons of men; and his heart was made like the beasts, and his dwelling was with the wild asses: they fed him with grass like oxen, and his body was wet with the dew of heaven; till he knew that the most high God ruled in the kingdom of men, and that he appointeth over it whomsoever he will.

22 And thou his son, O Belshazzar, hast not humbled thine heart, though thou knewest all this;

23 But hast lifted up thyself against the Lord of heaven; and they have brought

the vessels of his house before thee, and thou, and thy lords, thy wives, and thy concubines, have drunk wine in them; and thou hast praised the gods of silver, and gold, of brass, iron, wood, and stone, which see not, nor hear, nor know: and the God in whose hand thy breath is, and whose are all thy ways, hast thou not glorified:

24 Then was the part of the hand sent from him; and this writing was written.

25 And this is the writing that was written, Mene, Mene, Tekel, Upharsin.

26 This is the interpretation of the thing: Mene; God hath numbered thy kingdom, and finished it.

27 Tekel; Thou art weighed in the balances, and art found wanting.

28 Peres; Thy kingdom is divided, and given to the Medes and Persians.

29 Then commanded Belshazzar, and they clothed Daniel with scarlet, and put a chain of gold about his neck, and made a proclamation concerning him, that he should be the third ruler in the kingdom.

30 In that night was Belshazzar the king of the Chaldeans slain.

31 And Darius the Median took the kingdom, being about threescore and two

years old.

It's all about Faith
Daniel chapter 6
Good morning from Arizona

Some interesting things have transpired over the last few days. Not so long ago two very fine people did my wife and I a very good turn in the name of Christ. Yesterday we had a chance to pass on that generosity to someone in great need. Losing a wife and daughter to a terrible disease I know well the pain incurred and the physiological effect it can have on a family. It is my hope those two wonderful people who were so generous to my wife and myself will continue to receive Gods blessing for their good deeds.
In my research of late I have had the opportunity to study many of the early Christian men who were responsible for the Christian empire moving forward. It seems I never get enough learning in this area and it also seems like many others I have spent most of my life ignorant of the incredible strain and growth pains of Christianity. War after war was fought in the name of one thing or another and

Christianity was no different except for the fact God owns Heaven and earth and has a plan for saving mankind from himself.

Not long ago I read "If there were no sin, there would be no war". How beautifully simple and true that statement is. Is Christianity love? Yes it is, but we must remember it has also had to undergo the strain and birth of life just as any baby would. If not for Christ it may have died long ago. If not for Gods love of man it would have miscarried as a baby in the womb. Those things we read of from Genesis on are the growing pains that were necessary to finally arrive where we are today. We are flawed and imperfect, but we do know of God and most of know we now have a choice to accept or reject the Christ. The ground of this world is soaked in the blood of believers who would not submit to the lies and treachery of Satan and his angels. Has the fight been worth it? You tell me

Chapter 6
Daniel in the lion's den

1 It pleased Darius to set over the kingdom an hundred and twenty princes, which should be over the whole kingdom;
2 And over these three presidents; of whom Daniel was first: that the princes might give accounts unto them, and the king should have no damage.
3 Then this Daniel was preferred above the presidents and princes, because an excellent spirit was in him; and the king thought to set him over the whole realm.
4 Then the presidents and princes sought to find occasion against Daniel concerning the kingdom; but they could find none occasion nor fault; forasmuch as he was faithful, neither was there any error or fault found in him.
5 Then said these men, We shall not find any occasion against this Daniel, except we find it against him concerning the law of his God.
6 Then these presidents and princes assembled together to the king, and said thus unto him, King Darius, live for ever.

7 All the presidents of the kingdom, the governors, and the princes, the counsellors, and the captains, have consulted together to establish a royal statute, and to make a firm decree, that whosoever shall ask a petition of any God or man for thirty days, save of thee, O king, he shall be cast into the den of lions.
8 Now, O king, establish the decree, and sign the writing, that it be not changed, according to the law of the Medes and Persians, which altereth not.
9 Wherefore king Darius signed the writing and the decree.
10 Now when Daniel knew that the writing was signed, he went into his house; and his windows being open in his chamber toward Jerusalem, he kneeled upon his knees three times a day, and prayed, and gave thanks before his God, as he did aforetime.
11 Then these men assembled, and found Daniel praying and making supplication before his God.
12 Then they came near, and spake before the king concerning the king's decree; Hast thou not signed a decree, that every man that shall ask a petition of any God or man within thirty days, save

of thee, O king, shall be cast into the den of lions? The king answered and said, The thing is true, according to the law of the Medes and Persians, which altereth not.

13 Then answered they and said before the king, That Daniel, which is of the children of the captivity of Judah, regardeth not thee, O king, nor the decree that thou hast signed, but maketh his petition three times a day.

14 Then the king, when he heard these words, was sore displeased with himself, and set his heart on Daniel to deliver him: and he laboured till the going down of the sun to deliver him.

15 Then these men assembled unto the king, and said unto the king, Know, O king, that the law of the Medes and Persians is, That no decree nor statute which the king establisheth may be changed.

16 Then the king commanded, and they brought Daniel, and cast him into the den of lions. Now the king spake and said unto Daniel, Thy God whom thou servest continually, he will deliver thee.

17 And a stone was brought, and laid upon the mouth of the den; and the king

sealed it with his own signet, and with the signet of his lords; that the purpose might not be changed concerning Daniel.

18 Then the king went to his palace, and passed the night fasting: neither were instruments of musick brought before him: and his sleep went from him.

19 Then the king arose very early in the morning, and went in haste unto the den of lions.

20 And when he came to the den, he cried with a lamentable voice unto Daniel: and the king spake and said to Daniel, O Daniel, servant of the living God, is thy God, whom thou servest continually, able to deliver thee from the lions?

21 Then said Daniel unto the king, O king, live for ever.

22 My God hath sent his angel, and hath shut the lions' mouths, that they have not hurt me: forasmuch as before him innocency was found in me; and also before thee, O king, have I done no hurt.

23 Then was the king exceedingly glad for him, and commanded that they should take Daniel up out of the den. So Daniel was taken up out of the den, and no manner of hurt was found upon him, because he believed in his God.

24 And the king commanded, and they brought those men which had accused Daniel, and they cast them into the den of lions, them, their children, and their wives; and the lions had the mastery of them, and brake all their bones in pieces or ever they came at the bottom of the den.
25 Then king Darius wrote unto all people, nations, and languages, that dwell in all the earth; Peace be multiplied unto you.
26 I make a decree, That in every dominion of my kingdom men tremble and fear before the God of Daniel: for he is the living God, and stedfast for ever, and his kingdom that which shall not be destroyed, and his dominion shall be even unto the end.
27 He delivereth and rescueth, and he worketh signs and wonders in heaven and in earth, who hath delivered Daniel from the power of the lions.
28 So this Daniel prospered in the reign of Darius, and in the reign of Cyrus the Persian.

It's all about Faith
Daniel chapter 7
Good morning from the Deserts of the Southwest

Thursday morning and I am up very early in preparation for today's lesson which I must admit is quite interesting and informative and at the same time a test of my ability to explain it clearly. But I shall try and so let us proceed.

Ok, today we are reading chapter 7 in the book of Daniel and in my research of this material (which I might add comes from several sources, one of which is the "The Wycliffe Bible Commentary") I found some interesting points. This dream of Daniels was in the first year of the new ruler of Babylon and in those days it was customary to immediately write dreams down so as not to forget any of the details. In his dream "Ruah" meaning the spirit of the wind blew over the Great Sea (Mediterranean) and from the sea came four great beasts. All of which are similar and all are brutal in their power. Research suggests these beasts were the future ruling nations (If I may I will share here these few verses cover almost the same material as the book of Revelation which I find most interesting.) The Lion is of course Babylon, the Bear is Medo-Persian, and the Leopard is the power passed on to the Roman Empire and is to remain until the destruction of the Anti-Christ. The forth beast and by far the most terrible is the one who produces the "Little-Horn". It is suggested this may well be the Roman Empire which is to last into the last days of Gentile domination.

It is interesting to note here that in the end times all of these ruling nations (which are by the way Gentile) will be taken over by the Anti-Christ. Also it is believed that the ten nations that come together will not be formed by the Anti-Christ but will be absorbed by him. The little horn mentioned will be the Anti-Christ and he will be all beautiful, intelligent, and a bit different. His rein will be short and in the end brutal, but he will fall to the Christ. We can see by reading these verses that the complexity of this dream and the interpretation of it would cause Daniel to keep it to himself. Also I believe he did see the Christ in this dream or perhaps Gabriel the angel.

Chapter 7
Daniels Dream

1 In the first year of Belshazzar king of Babylon Daniel had a dream and visions of his head upon his bed: then he wrote the dream, and told the sum of the matters.

2 Daniel spake and said, I saw in my vision by night, and, behold, the four winds of the heaven strove upon the great sea.

3 And four great beasts came up from the sea, diverse one from another.

4 The first was like a lion, and had eagle's wings: I beheld till the wings thereof were plucked, and it was lifted up from the earth, and made stand upon the feet as a man, and a man's heart was given to it.

5 And behold another beast, a second, like to a bear, and it raised up itself on one side, and it had three ribs in the mouth of it between the teeth of it: and they said thus unto it, Arise, devour much flesh.

6 After this I beheld, and lo another, like a leopard, which had upon the back of it

four wings of a fowl; the beast had also four heads; and dominion was given to it.
7 After this I saw in the night visions, and behold a fourth beast, dreadful and terrible, and strong exceedingly; and it had great iron teeth: it devoured and brake in pieces, and stamped the residue with the feet of it: and it was diverse from all the beasts that were before it; and it had ten horns.
8 I considered the horns, and, behold, there came up among them another little horn, before whom there were three of the first horns plucked up by the roots: and, behold, in this horn were eyes like the eyes of man, and a mouth speaking great things.
9 I beheld till the thrones were cast down, and the Ancient of days did sit, whose garment was white as snow, and the hair of his head like the pure wool: his throne was like the fiery flame, and his wheels as burning fire.
10 A fiery stream issued and came forth from before him: thousand thousands ministered unto him, and ten thousand times ten thousand stood before him: the judgment was set, and the books were opened.

11 I beheld then because of the voice of the great words which the horn spake: I beheld even till the beast was slain, and his body destroyed, and given to the burning flame.

12 As concerning the rest of the beasts, they had their dominion taken away: yet their lives were prolonged for a season and time.

13 I saw in the night visions, and, behold, one like the Son of man came with the clouds of heaven, and came to the Ancient of days, and they brought him near before him.

14 And there was given him dominion, and glory, and a kingdom, that all people, nations, and languages, should serve him: his dominion is an everlasting dominion, which shall not pass away, and his kingdom that which shall not be destroyed.

15 I Daniel was grieved in my spirit in the midst of my body, and the visions of my head troubled me.

16 I came near unto one of them that stood by, and asked him the truth of all this. So he told me, and made me know the interpretation of the things.

17 These great beasts, which are four, are four kings, which shall arise out of the earth.
18 But the saints of the most High shall take the kingdom, and possess the kingdom for ever, even for ever and ever.
19 Then I would know the truth of the fourth beast, which was diverse from all the others, exceeding dreadful, whose teeth were of iron, and his nails of brass; which devoured, brake in pieces, and stamped the residue with his feet;
20 And of the ten horns that were in his head, and of the other which came up, and before whom three fell; even of that horn that had eyes, and a mouth that spake very great things, whose look was more stout than his fellows.
21 I beheld, and the same horn made war with the saints, and prevailed against them;
22 Until the Ancient of days came, and judgment was given to the saints of the most High; and the time came that the saints possessed the kingdom.
23 Thus he said, The fourth beast shall be the fourth kingdom upon earth, which shall be diverse from all kingdoms, and

shall devour the whole earth, and shall tread it down, and break it in pieces.

24 And the ten horns out of this kingdom are ten kings that shall arise: and another shall rise after them; and he shall be diverse from the first, and he shall subdue three kings.

25 And he shall speak great words against the most High, and shall wear out the saints of the most High, and think to change times and laws: and they shall be given into his hand until a time and times and the dividing of time.

26 But the judgment shall sit, and they shall take away his dominion, to consume and to destroy it unto the end.

27 And the kingdom and dominion, and the greatness of the kingdom under the whole heaven, shall be given to the people of the saints of the most High, whose kingdom is an everlasting kingdom, and all dominions shall serve and obey him.

28 Hitherto is the end of the matter. As for me Daniel, my cogitations much troubled me, and my countenance changed in me: but I kept the matter in my heart.

It's all about Faith
Daniel chapter 8
Good morning from our house

Getting a rather late start this morning due to Arthur keeping me up most of the night. There are times when pain is just so inconvenient, but we go on anyway and there is the pleasure in not giving in. So I bid you a good morning from the desert.

Ok, this morning as we read chapter 8 we are in one of the most important, beautiful and historical, and I might add accurate writings of the Bible. This vision Daniel had is so powerful and clear and historically correct as we will see as we proceed.
First let me share with you the research on this chapter indicates that the Ram, and Goat are form animals of gentle make up. This is so because both were not cruel to the Jews at least not as the "Bear, Lion, and Leopard was". Also it is important to note that this vision was directly related to the fact that the Jews in exile needed to know that the Lords

promise of restoration to their homeland was going to come about.

The Ram here is the Medes (one horn) and the other horn is the Persians. These two came to hate one another. The goat that arrives on the scene with the horn between its eyes is the powerful Alexzander from Greece and he will crush the other two. The broken horn is the death of Alexander at the age of 33 in Babylon.

We see here that Gabriel the angel is involved in this powerful vision as well and speaks directly to Daniel explaining the dream. The daily pagan sacrifices in the temple are mentioned as well. Remember, all of these things we read about came to pass exactly as noted in this chapter and this should erase any doubt that one might have concerning whether or not God is real.

Chapter 8
Denial's vision of the ram and the goat.

1In the third year of the reign of king Belshazzar a vision appeared unto me, even unto me Daniel, after that which appeared unto me at the first.

2 And I saw in a vision; and it came to pass, when I saw, that I was at Shushan in the palace, which is in the province of Elam; and I saw in a vision, and I was by the river of Ulai.

3 Then I lifted up mine eyes, and saw, and, behold, there stood before the river a ram which had two horns: and the two horns were high; but one was higher than the other, and the higher came up last.

4 I saw the ram pushing westward, and northward, and southward; so that no beasts might stand before him, neither was there any that could deliver out of his hand; but he did according to his will, and became great.

5 And as I was considering, behold, an he goat came from the west on the face of the whole earth, and touched not the ground: and the goat had a notable horn between his eyes.

6 And he came to the ram that had two horns, which I had seen standing before the river, and ran unto him in the fury of his power.

7 And I saw him come close unto the ram, and he was moved with choler against him, and smote the ram, and brake his two horns: and there was no

power in the ram to stand before him, but he cast him down to the ground, and stamped upon him: and there was none that could deliver the ram out of his hand.

8 Therefore the he goat waxed very great: and when he was strong, the great horn was broken; and for it came up four notable ones toward the four winds of heaven.

9 And out of one of them came forth a little horn, which waxed exceeding great, toward the south, and toward the east, and toward the pleasant land.

10 And it waxed great, even to the host of heaven; and it cast down some of the host and of the stars to the ground, and stamped upon them.

11 Yea, he magnified himself even to the prince of the host, and by him the daily sacrifice was taken away, and the place of the sanctuary was cast down.

12 And an host was given him against the daily sacrifice by reason of transgression, and it cast down the truth to the ground; and it practised, and prospered.

13 Then I heard one saint speaking, and another saint said unto that certain saint which spake, How long shall be the vision concerning the daily sacrifice, and the

transgression of desolation, to give both the sanctuary and the host to be trodden under foot?

14 And he said unto me, Unto two thousand and three hundred days; then shall the sanctuary be cleansed.

15 And it came to pass, when I, even I Daniel, had seen the vision, and sought for the meaning, then, behold, there stood before me as the appearance of a man.

16 And I heard a man's voice between the banks of Ulai, which called, and said, Gabriel, make this man to understand the vision.

17 So he came near where I stood: and when he came, I was afraid, and fell upon my face: but he said unto me, Understand, O son of man: for at the time of the end shall be the vision.

18 Now as he was speaking with me, I was in a deep sleep on my face toward the ground: but he touched me, and set me upright.

19 And he said, Behold, I will make thee know what shall be in the last end of the indignation: for at the time appointed the end shall be.

20 The ram which thou sawest having two horns are the kings of Media and Persia.
21 And the rough goat is the king of Grecia: and the great horn that is between his eyes is the first king.
22 Now that being broken, whereas four stood up for it, four kingdoms shall stand up out of the nation, but not in his power.
23 And in the latter time of their kingdom, when the transgressors are come to the full, a king of fierce countenance, and understanding dark sentences, shall stand up.
24 And his power shall be mighty, but not by his own power: and he shall destroy wonderfully, and shall prosper, and practise, and shall destroy the mighty and the holy people.
25 And through his policy also he shall cause craft to prosper in his hand; and he shall magnify himself in his heart, and by peace shall destroy many: he shall also stand up against the Prince of princes; but he shall be broken without hand.
26 And the vision of the evening and the morning which was told is true: wherefore shut thou up the vision; for it shall be for many days.

27 And I Daniel fainted, and was sick certain days; afterward I rose up, and did the king's business; and I was astonished at the vision, but none understood it.

It's all about Faith
Daniel chapter 9
Good morning friends from the world over

Ordinarily I start the days study off with a personal comment of some kind, but this chapter 9 is so very important and I might add a bit complicated that I thought we might get right to it. The reading and research of this chapter was very involved and page after page of the meanings of almost every word by Bible scholars and historians made me realize after a considerable time of study that to get to specific in my explanation of this reading would be an oversimplification. That is not to say we cannot understand what is going on but it is to say that the things Daniel says and sees are of such importance that we must just take what we read at face value. Having said that let us begin and trust God will give us understanding.

Ok, this prayer takes place in the first year of the rule of general Darius (king over Babylon only) and the 67th year of Daniels exile in that country. This is about 50 years before the final destruction of Jerusalem in 586 BC. Daniel knew the time of the destruction Jerusalem was at hand because the Lord had said "I will punish the king of Babylon" and this had already happened.

Notice that Daniel confesses both his sins and the sins of Israel before the lord, and he also reminds the Lord these are His people and this is His city. Pleading for saving the city and the people. Gabriel comes to his side in person and tells Daniel that he is held in great regard (wouldn't it be nice to have Gods own angel say that to us?) and explains what is to come. The Christ, his crucifixion, and things that have not yet taken place. So, we now have a glimpse of the power and importance of this prayer.

I would only add that Daniel was given exceptional understanding and his visions and words have an effect on the future in that all have been proven to be true.
If everyone would lite but one little candle what a bright world this would be.
Have a great weekend. See you on Monday.
Peace.

Chapter 9
Daniel Prays

1 In the first year of Darius the son of Ahasuerus, of the seed of the Medes, which was made king over the realm of the Chaldeans;
2 In the first year of his reign I Daniel understood by books the number of the years, whereof the word of the Lord came to Jeremiah the prophet, that he would accomplish seventy years in the desolations of Jerusalem.
3 And I set my face unto the Lord God, to seek by prayer and supplications, with fasting, and sackcloth, and ashes:

4 And I prayed unto the Lord my God, and made my confession, and said, O Lord, the great and dreadful God, keeping the covenant and mercy to them that love him, and to them that keep his commandments;
5 We have sinned, and have committed iniquity, and have done wickedly, and have rebelled, even by departing from thy precepts and from thy judgments:
6 Neither have we hearkened unto thy servants the prophets, which spake in thy name to our kings, our princes, and our fathers, and to all the people of the land.
7 O Lord, righteousness belongeth unto thee, but unto us confusion of faces, as at this day; to the men of Judah, and to the inhabitants of Jerusalem, and unto all Israel, that are near, and that are far off, through all the countries whither thou hast driven them, because of their trespass that they have trespassed against thee.
8 O Lord, to us belongeth confusion of face, to our kings, to our princes, and to our fathers, because we have sinned against thee.

9 To the Lord our God belong mercies and forgivenesses, though we have rebelled against him;

10 Neither have we obeyed the voice of the Lord our God, to walk in his laws, which he set before us by his servants the prophets.

11 Yea, all Israel have transgressed thy law, even by departing, that they might not obey thy voice; therefore the curse is poured upon us, and the oath that is written in the law of Moses the servant of God, because we have sinned against him.

12 And he hath confirmed his words, which he spake against us, and against our judges that judged us, by bringing upon us a great evil: for under the whole heaven hath not been done as hath been done upon Jerusalem.

13 As it is written in the law of Moses, all this evil is come upon us: yet made we not our prayer before the Lord our God, that we might turn from our iniquities, and understand thy truth.

14 Therefore hath the Lord watched upon the evil, and brought it upon us: for the

Lord our God is righteous in all his works which he doeth: for we obeyed not his voice.

15 And now, O Lord our God, that hast brought thy people forth out of the land of Egypt with a mighty hand, and hast gotten thee renown, as at this day; we have sinned, we have done wickedly.

16 O Lord, according to all thy righteousness, I beseech thee, let thine anger and thy fury be turned away from thy city Jerusalem, thy holy mountain: because for our sins, and for the iniquities of our fathers, Jerusalem and thy people are become a reproach to all that are about us.

17 Now therefore, O our God, hear the prayer of thy servant, and his supplications, and cause thy face to shine upon thy sanctuary that is desolate, for the Lord's sake.

18 O my God, incline thine ear, and hear; open thine eyes, and behold our desolations, and the city which is called by thy name: for we do not present our supplications before thee for our

righteousnesses, but for thy great mercies.

19 O Lord, hear; O Lord, forgive; O Lord, hearken and do; defer not, for thine own sake, O my God: for thy city and thy people are called by thy name.

20 And whiles I was speaking, and praying, and confessing my sin and the sin of my people Israel, and presenting my supplication before the Lord my God for the holy mountain of my God;

21 Yea, whiles I was speaking in prayer, even the man Gabriel, whom I had seen in the vision at the beginning, being caused to fly swiftly, touched me about the time of the evening oblation.

22 And he informed me, and talked with me, and said, O Daniel, I am now come forth to give thee skill and understanding.

23 At the beginning of thy supplications the commandment came forth, and I am come to shew thee; for thou art greatly beloved: therefore understand the matter, and consider the vision.

24 Seventy weeks are determined upon thy people and upon thy holy city, to finish the transgression, and to make an end of

sins, and to make reconciliation for iniquity, and to bring in everlasting righteousness, and to seal up the vision and prophecy, and to anoint the most Holy.

25 Know therefore and understand, that from the going forth of the commandment to restore and to build Jerusalem unto the Messiah the Prince shall be seven weeks, and threescore and two weeks: the street shall be built again, and the wall, even in troublous times.

26 And after threescore and two weeks shall Messiah be cut off, but not for himself: and the people of the prince that shall come shall destroy the city and the sanctuary; and the end thereof shall be with a flood, and unto the end of the war desolations are determined.

27 And he shall confirm the covenant with many for one week: and in the midst of the week he shall cause the sacrifice and the oblation to cease, and for the overspreading of abominations he shall make it desolate, even until the consummation, and that determined shall be poured upon the desolate.

It's all about Faith
Daniel chapter 10
Good morning friends from Africa and the rest of the world

Well, here we are up before the sun on a Monday morning in America with God providing yet another chance to "get it right".
About the greeting this morning. I have so many friends from around the world reading with me each day that I thought it appropriate to greet each of your countries as we go along. With that said let us begin this weeks lessons.

Ok, I have started this writing several times and I believe after reading the research and scripture we need to take the chapter as it was written.
It seems that Daniel was fasting (it is thought the reason may have been because the work on the temple had for some reason come to a standstill.) and was in his fourth week of doing so and was just now sitting by the river Tigris (It

is interesting to note this river runs from southeastern Turkey through Iraq.) with friends when he looks up and standing above the water is a man. The ground shakes and all of those with Daniel run and hide. (Again, I found there is a difference of opinion here as just who this man was. His description was much like that in Revelation, but again it is thought by some it could be Gabriel.) We read of the word Uphaz the man has around his waist. (This is very pure gold and significant as it could be as Christ might dress considering his position and authority.)

Daniel is overcome by the very presence of this man and must be helped to stand and even speak. Daniel listens and the man closes with the statement of he must take his leave to fight against Persia and that soon the Prince of Greece (Alexander) will come.

I found it extremely interesting to read that the man said " no one supports me against them, but Michael" was used in this writing of scripture indicating there are many in heaven.

Have a great day and I will see you tomorrow. Remember if everyone would lite but one little candle what a bright world this would be.

Peace.

My dear friends, we, all of us are responsible for our own salvation. We must at some time in our lives make the choice of believing or not in God. That is why I ask you to read for yourselves and learn about those things that are so important to our lives. We can all be led to hell by our good intentions and letting others do our thinking for us. Do not let that happen to you.

Chapter 10
Daniels vision and the man

1 In the third year of Cyrus king of Persia a thing was revealed unto Daniel, whose name was called Belteshazzar; and the thing was true, but the time appointed was long: and he understood the thing, and had understanding of the vision.
2 In those days I Daniel was mourning three full weeks.

3 I ate no pleasant bread, neither came flesh nor wine in my mouth, neither did I anoint myself at all, till three whole weeks were fulfilled.

4 And in the four and twentieth day of the first month, as I was by the side of the great river, which is Hiddekel;

5 Then I lifted up mine eyes, and looked, and behold a certain man clothed in linen, whose loins were girded with fine gold of Uphaz:

6 His body also was like the beryl, and his face as the appearance of lightning, and his eyes as lamps of fire, and his arms and his feet like in colour to polished brass, and the voice of his words like the voice of a multitude.

7 And I Daniel alone saw the vision: for the men that were with me saw not the vision; but a great quaking fell upon them, so that they fled to hide themselves.

8 Therefore I was left alone, and saw this great vision, and there remained no strength in me: for my comeliness was turned in me into corruption, and I retained no strength.

9 Yet heard I the voice of his words: and when I heard the voice of his words, then was I in a deep sleep on my face, and my face toward the ground.

10 And, behold, an hand touched me, which set me upon my knees and upon the palms of my hands.

11 And he said unto me, O Daniel, a man greatly beloved, understand the words that I speak unto thee, and stand upright: for unto thee am I now sent. And when he had spoken this word unto me, I stood trembling.

12 Then said he unto me, Fear not, Daniel: for from the first day that thou didst set thine heart to understand, and to chasten thyself before thy God, thy words were heard, and I am come for thy words.

13 But the prince of the kingdom of Persia withstood me one and twenty days: but, lo, Michael, one of the chief princes, came to help me; and I remained there with the kings of Persia.

14 Now I am come to make thee understand what shall befall thy people in the latter days: for yet the vision is for many days.

15 And when he had spoken such words unto me, I set my face toward the ground, and I became dumb.

16 And, behold, one like the similitude of the sons of men touched my lips: then I opened my mouth, and spake, and said unto him that stood before me, O my lord, by the vision my sorrows are turned upon me, and I have retained no strength.

17 For how can the servant of this my lord talk with this my lord? for as for me, straightway there remained no strength in me, neither is there breath left in me.

18 Then there came again and touched me one like the appearance of a man, and he strengthened me,

19 And said, O man greatly beloved, fear not: peace be unto thee, be strong, yea, be strong. And when he had spoken unto me, I was strengthened, and said, Let my lord speak; for thou hast strengthened me.

20 Then said he, Knowest thou wherefore I come unto thee? and now will I return to fight with the prince of Persia: and when I am gone forth, lo, the prince of Grecia shall come.

21 But I will shew thee that which is noted in the scripture of truth: and there is none that holdeth with me in these things, but Michael your prince.

It's all about Faith
Daniel Chapter 11
Good morning Nicaragua and the rest of the world.

Slept in this morning until about 0500. I do that on occasion just to remind myself that after 60 years of work I can do as I please.
I am very glad to be able to spend this time with you each day for together we read and learn of God. There are many who are far more learned than I of that I am sure, but I do this with a glad heart and because I was appointed to do so. I believe those who seek God and study HIS word will be given the understanding they need to find the gate that leads to HIS house. So let us begin.

Ok, today as we read chapter 11 of the book of Daniel together we see in his vision that there is much war. This chapter speaks of the king of the south, Egypt, and the king of the north, Syria. The material in this chapter covers a great deal of territory. In the opening line of this chapter we find that Daniel supports the king of the city of Babylon (Darius) who was kind to the Jews there in exile. Then the text goes on to tell of wars between the North and South and of the Persians infuriating the nation of Greece and of Alexander the Great. We then read of the North and South coming together to fight against another king, but to no avail. We also read of the "Ships of Chittim". These are the maritime war ships of the Mediterranean coastlands. In verse 31 we see for the first time the appearance of the Antichrist (Roman king). He arrives on the scene with flattery and lies, but there will be people that know who he is even though he will deceive many. Those who know who he is will speak out against him and stand up for their God and a great many will die for it. They nonetheless will not be silenced and will continue to hold their heads up in the face of his terrible actions. Let me pause here and share with you that I read that this Antichrist will quite obviously not be a gentile. It would not be possible for a gentile to mislead and fool the Jewish people. This Antichrist goes on to win and rule until he meets his demise.

We should understand the war Daniel sees is in the future he sees in his own armies' power because he would not understand the machines of our modern day war equipment. There is much more that should be said about this chapter but space does not permit it.

Thank you for being here and remember it takes just a tiny spark to lite a candle and if everyone would lite but one what a bright world this would be.

Until tomorrow.

Love you guys.

Chapter 11
Northern and Southern Kings

1 Also I in the first year of Darius the Mede, even I, stood to confirm and to strengthen him.

2 And now will I shew thee the truth. Behold, there shall stand up yet three kings in Persia; and the fourth shall be far richer than they all: and by his strength through his riches he shall stir up all against the realm of Grecia.
3 And a mighty king shall stand up, that shall rule with great dominion, and do according to his will.
4 And when he shall stand up, his kingdom shall be broken, and shall be divided toward the four winds of heaven; and not to his posterity, nor according to his dominion which he ruled: for his kingdom shall be plucked up, even for others beside those.
5 And the king of the south shall be strong, and one of his princes; and he shall be strong above him, and have dominion; his dominion shall be a great dominion.
6 And in the end of years they shall join themselves together; for the king's daughter of the south shall come to the king of the north to make an agreement: but she shall not retain the power of the arm; neither shall he stand, nor his arm: but she shall be given up, and they that

brought her, and he that begat her, and he that strengthened her in these times.
7 But out of a branch of her roots shall one stand up in his estate, which shall come with an army, and shall enter into the fortress of the king of the north, and shall deal against them, and shall prevail:
8 And shall also carry captives into Egypt their gods, with their princes, and with their precious vessels of silver and of gold; and he shall continue more years than the king of the north.
9 So the king of the south shall come into his kingdom, and shall return into his own land.
10 But his sons shall be stirred up, and shall assemble a multitude of great forces: and one shall certainly come, and overflow, and pass through: then shall he return, and be stirred up, even to his fortress.
11 And the king of the south shall be moved with choler, and shall come forth and fight with him, even with the king of the north: and he shall set forth a great multitude; but the multitude shall be given into his hand.
12 And when he hath taken away the multitude, his heart shall be lifted up; and

he shall cast down many ten thousands: but he shall not be strengthened by it.

13 For the king of the north shall return, and shall set forth a multitude greater than the former, and shall certainly come after certain years with a great army and with much riches.

14 And in those times there shall many stand up against the king of the south: also the robbers of thy people shall exalt themselves to establish the vision; but they shall fall.

15 So the king of the north shall come, and cast up a mount, and take the most fenced cities: and the arms of the south shall not withstand, neither his chosen people, neither shall there be any strength to withstand.

16 But he that cometh against him shall do according to his own will, and none shall stand before him: and he shall stand in the glorious land, which by his hand shall be consumed.

17 He shall also set his face to enter with the strength of his whole kingdom, and upright ones with him; thus shall he do: and he shall give him the daughter of women, corrupting her: but she shall not stand on his side, neither be for him.

18 After this shall he turn his face unto the isles, and shall take many: but a prince for his own behalf shall cause the reproach offered by him to cease; without his own reproach he shall cause it to turn upon him.

19 Then he shall turn his face toward the fort of his own land: but he shall stumble and fall, and not be found.

20 Then shall stand up in his estate a raiser of taxes in the glory of the kingdom: but within few days he shall be destroyed, neither in anger, nor in battle.

21 And in his estate shall stand up a vile person, to whom they shall not give the honour of the kingdom: but he shall come in peaceably, and obtain the kingdom by flatteries.

22 And with the arms of a flood shall they be overflown from before him, and shall be broken; yea, also the prince of the covenant.

23 And after the league made with him he shall work deceitfully: for he shall come up, and shall become strong with a small people.

24 He shall enter peaceably even upon the fattest places of the province; and he shall do that which his fathers have not

done, nor his fathers' fathers; he shall scatter among them the prey, and spoil, and riches: yea, and he shall forecast his devices against the strong holds, even for a time.

25 And he shall stir up his power and his courage against the king of the south with a great army; and the king of the south shall be stirred up to battle with a very great and mighty army; but he shall not stand: for they shall forecast devices against him.

26 Yea, they that feed of the portion of his meat shall destroy him, and his army shall overflow: and many shall fall down slain.

27 And both of these kings' hearts shall be to do mischief, and they shall speak lies at one table; but it shall not prosper: for yet the end shall be at the time appointed.

28 Then shall he return into his land with great riches; and his heart shall be against the holy covenant; and he shall do exploits, and return to his own land.

29 At the time appointed he shall return, and come toward the south; but it shall not be as the former, or as the latter.

30 For the ships of Chittim shall come against him: therefore he shall be grieved, and return, and have indignation against the holy covenant: so shall he do; he shall even return, and have intelligence with them that forsake the holy covenant.

31 And arms shall stand on his part, and they shall pollute the sanctuary of strength, and shall take away the daily sacrifice, and they shall place the abomination that maketh desolate.

32 And such as do wickedly against the covenant shall he corrupt by flatteries: but the people that do know their God shall be strong, and do exploits.

33 And they that understand among the people shall instruct many: yet they shall fall by the sword, and by flame, by captivity, and by spoil, many days.

34 Now when they shall fall, they shall be holpen with a little help: but many shall cleave to them with flatteries.

35 And some of them of understanding shall fall, to try them, and to purge, and to make them white, even to the time of the end: because it is yet for a time appointed.

36 And the king shall do according to his will; and he shall exalt himself, and magnify himself above every god, and shall speak marvellous things against the God of gods, and shall prosper till the indignation be accomplished: for that that is determined shall be done.
37 Neither shall he regard the God of his fathers, nor the desire of women, nor regard any god: for he shall magnify himself above all.
38 But in his estate shall he honour the God of forces: and a god whom his fathers knew not shall he honour with gold, and silver, and with precious stones, and pleasant things.
39 Thus shall he do in the most strong holds with a strange god, whom he shall acknowledge and increase with glory: and he shall cause them to rule over many, and shall divide the land for gain.
40 And at the time of the end shall the king of the south push at him: and the king of the north shall come against him like a whirlwind, with chariots, and with horsemen, and with many ships; and he shall enter into the countries, and shall overflow and pass over.

41 He shall enter also into the glorious land, and many countries shall be overthrown: but these shall escape out of his hand, even Edom, and Moab, and the chief of the children of Ammon.

42 He shall stretch forth his hand also upon the countries: and the land of Egypt shall not escape.

43 But he shall have power over the treasures of gold and of silver, and over all the precious things of Egypt: and the Libyans and the Ethiopians shall be at his steps.

44 But tidings out of the east and out of the north shall trouble him: therefore he shall go forth with great fury to destroy, and utterly to make away many.

45 And he shall plant the tabernacles of his palace between the seas in the glorious holy mountain; yet he shall come to his end, and none shall help him.

It's all about Faith
Daniel chapter 12
Good morning Europe and the rest of the world.

I stepped out the door this morning on my way to the office our little RV that sits just around the corner from the house to find it to be quite windy. It is however quite warm and comfortable this morning at 0500. My lovely wife of 32 years joins me on some mornings and we have coffee and toast together before doing our Bible work.

Today we bid farewell to the prophet Daniel and his visions. His work was very special and insightful teaching us a great deal about what has happened in the past and what is to come in the future for Israel and the rest of the world for that matter. So, let us begin this last chapter and learn of things to come.

Ok, this reading of chapter 12 of the "Book of Daniel" concerns the vision and prophecy of the "Great Tribulation of Israel" which is coming. The antichrist at that time will be causing war against Israel and God for that matter. This will be during the last three and one half years of his terror campaign. Gods angle Michael will at this time "stand-up" against the evil one. As we read this final chapter we need to keep in mind that all of this is in preparation for the coming of the Messiah, Jesus Christ. This will be a time of the waking of those that have been asleep throughout all the world waiting on the Lord. "Some will wake to everlasting life and some to everlasting shame and contempt" At that time the understanding of the prophecies will grow and wisdom will increase. This is indeed a time of Israel's trouble. We read of two angelic beings each standing on either side of the river and one dressed in linen standing above the water. It is assumed this person is the Christ and Daniel asks when this time of trouble will end. He is told to go his way and that the words written in the book are shut up and sealed until the time of the end. He is also told that many will be made white and tried, (tested and I assume tortured) and that the wicked will continue to be wicked and not understand, but the wise shall understand.

The beautiful ending to this book of Daniel. V13 "But go thou thy way till the end be: for thou shalt rest, and stand in thy lot at the end of the days". (Receive your inheritance.)

That closes the book of Daniel. The journey has been an exciting and beautiful learning experience.

Tomorrow we start our journey through the "Book of Hosea".

Thank you for joining me each morning for our ten minute walk with the Lord.

If everyone would lite but one little candle what a bright world this would be.

Peace.

Chapter 12
The Last Days

1 And at that time shall Michael stand up, the great prince which standeth for the children of thy people: and there shall be a time of trouble, such as never was since there was a nation even to that same time: and at that time thy people shall be delivered, every one that shall be found written in the book.

2 And many of them that sleep in the dust of the earth shall awake, some to everlasting life, and some to shame and everlasting contempt.

3 And they that be wise shall shine as the brightness of the firmament; and they that turn many to righteousness as the stars for ever and ever.

4 But thou, O Daniel, shut up the words, and seal the book, even to the time of the end: many shall run to and fro, and knowledge shall be increased.

5 Then I Daniel looked, and, behold, there stood other two, the one on this side of the bank of the river, and the other on that side of the bank of the river.

6 And one said to the man clothed in linen, which was upon the waters of the river, How long shall it be to the end of these wonders?

7 And I heard the man clothed in linen, which was upon the waters of the river, when he held up his right hand and his left hand unto heaven, and sware by him that liveth for ever that it shall be for a time, times, and an half; and when he shall have accomplished to scatter the power of the holy people, all these things shall be finished.

8 And I heard, but I understood not: then said I, O my Lord, what shall be the end of these things?

9 And he said, Go thy way, Daniel: for the words are closed up and sealed till the time of the end.

10 Many shall be purified, and made white, and tried; but the wicked shall do wickedly: and none of the wicked shall understand; but the wise shall understand.

11 And from the time that the daily sacrifice shall be taken away, and the abomination that maketh desolate set up, there shall be a thousand two hundred and ninety days.

12 Blessed is he that waiteth, and cometh to the thousand three hundred and five and thirty days.

13 But go thou thy way till the end be: for thou shalt rest, and stand in thy lot at the end of the days.

Thank you.
May Father God bless your days throughout the rest of your life and may peace and prosperity visit you each morning and evening.

Blessings

Printed in Dunstable, United Kingdom